The BIG BROCCOLI Book

THE
BIG
BROCCOLI
BOOK

· · · · · · · · · · · · · ·

Georgia Downard

RANDOM HOUSE NEW YORK

Copyright © 1992 by Georgia Downard
All rights reserved under International and Pan-American Copyright Conventions.
Published in the United States by Random House, Inc., New York, and simultaneously
in Canada by Random House of Canada Limited, Toronto.

Library of Congress Cataloging-in-Publication Data
Downard, Georgia.
The big broccoli book / Georgia Downard
p.   cm.
ISBN 0-679-74382-0
1. Cookery (Broccoli)   I. Title.
TX803.B66D68   1992
641.6'535—dc20   92-25555

Manufactured in the United States of America
98765432

Illustrations and book design by Lilly Langotsky

FOR MY CHILDREN, BENJAMIN AND EMILY,

THE LIGHT OF MY LIFE

"I do not like broccoli."
—President George Bush (March 1992)

"While others are gorging on chocolate,
I'm gladsomely crying, 'It's broccoli time.'"
—Roy Blount

ACKNOWLEDGMENTS

· ·

First, I would like to thank Jill Cohen for thinking of me when the subject of this book arose. We are all enriched by her inspiration and thorough professionalism.

Second, thanks to Rebecca Beuchler for her cheerful enthusiasm, tireless patience, and eagerness to assist in any way possible.

Third, thanks to Lilly Langotsky for her style and creativity.

Fourth but certainly not least, my heartfelt thanks to Zanne Zakroff and Diane Keitt for their encouragement and unwavering support during the writing of this book.

CONTENTS

. . . .

GRAINS AND PASTA

MEATLESS ENTRÉES

SIDE DISHES

SAUCES FOR BROCCOLI

INDEX

The
BIG
BROCCOLI
Book

A Word About Broccoli

. . . .

Despite President George Bush's publicly stated aversion to broccoli, this remarkable vegetable is served at our house at least four or five times a week. In fact, broccoli consumption throughout the United States is at an all-time high. It is one of the few vegetables my children will eat, and they never seem to tire of it: They enjoy it day in and day out, cooked or uncooked, hot or cold. I sometimes manage to sneak in a carrot or green bean, but must then suffer their complaints.

Lending credence to the adage "The apple does not fall far from the tree," I must acknowledge that broccoli is one of my favorite foods, too. Its beauty and versatility make it a pleasure to cook. Broccoli may easily be paired with pasta, grains, seafood, poultry, and dairy products. It can also stand on its own, garnished simply with a light dressing or crowned with a classic sauce and served as an elegant first course.

Broccoli, which originated in the warm areas around the Mediterranean and was first cultivated in Calabria, has long been a favorite of Italian cooks. Its name comes from an Italian word meaning a sprout or small nail. It was introduced into the United States as a commercial crop during the 1920s, being bought mostly by families of Italian heritage, primarily on the East and West coasts. Its popularity soon spread, and before long its commercial production increased dramatically. Broccoli production in the 1950s reached in excess of 150 million pounds. By 1965, that figure had doubled. Most broccoli now found at the market is grown in California and is harvested from February through December, but fortunately for the consumer, it is marketed year-round throughout most of the country and may be enjoyed daily.

The two most common types of broccoli (which belongs to the genus *Brassica*) are "heading"—similar to cauliflower and not widely marketed in this country—and "sprouting," the kind with which we are most familiar. Along with cabbage, cauliflower, and brussels sprouts, broccoli belongs to the family of vegetables known as Cruciferae, so named because of the cruciform shape of their blossoms. These vegetables are abundantly endowed with essential vitamins and minerals. They are low in both sodium and calories, and are virtually fat- and cholesterol-free. Broccoli is also a wonderful source of fiber.

Cruciferae vegetables are also rich in beta-carotene, a component of dietary vitamin A that has been found to be one of the antioxidants that may give some protection against cancer. An average serving of broccoli provides enough beta-carotene to meet the daily requirement of vitamin A.

The most astonishing fact about broccoli, however, was published in March 1992 by researchers at Johns Hopkins University. Their report states that broccoli and related vegetables contain a natural chemical called sulforaphane that boosts the production of an enzyme known to reduce carcinogens before they cause malignant changes in the body. Dr. Paul Talalay, the molecular pharmacologist who directed the research, said, however, that several years of research on both animals and humans would be needed before it could conclusively be stated that broccoli helps to prevent cancer. What the report does emphasize, however, is the importance of determining what it is we are eating and the ability to isolate the chemicals in our food that help protect us against toxins and carcinogens. Identifying the presence of sulforaphane in broccoli and related vegetables may be why people who eat large amounts of these vegetables have a significantly reduced risk of cancer compared with those who avoid such foods.

So whether you're eating broccoli for its remarkable health benefits or simply because you like it, I hope the recipes in this book enable you to serve and enjoy it every day of the week.

BUYING

When purchasing broccoli, look for unblemished, firm, and compact clusters. The heads should smell fresh; the florets may range in color from dark to purplish green. Leaves should be crisp, and stalks smooth. If broccoli has yellowing blossoms and open buds, it is old and should be avoided.

STORING

Rinse the broccoli in water, shake off the excess moisture, and transfer to a plastic bag. Refrigerate until ready to use.

Broccoli is at its best when eaten soon after purchase. To reduce the loss of nutrients, particularly vitamin C, do not separate into florets, cut, or peel stalks until ready to cook. Once broccoli comes into contact with oxygen, vitamin C is destroyed. The skin or peel on vegetables acts to protect them from this loss, so the less surface exposed to oxygen the fewer vitamins are lost.

COOKING

For best results, cut broccoli into florets about 2 inches long and peel the stems. The stalks should also be peeled, sliced, cut into matchsticks, or diced. If only the florets are to be used, reserve the stalks for soups, purees, or sauces. Cutting broccoli this way reduces the cooking time to a minimum. Brief cooking brightens the color and brings out the flavor. Overcooking dulls both color and taste.

Green vegetables lose their vivid color if cooked longer than 6 to 8 minutes in a covered pan. This is because the acid they contain is released into the cooking water and converts the bright green chlorophyll into a drab olive. To prevent this, cook the broccoli, uncovered, in a large amount of water: This dilutes the acids and allows them to escape.

Steaming—cooking in water vapor rather than in the water itself—preserves all the essential nutrients in broccoli. Steamed broccoli retains 80 percent of vitamin C; boiled broccoli only 33 percent. Be sure to distribute the vegetables evenly on the steamer rack, adding it to the pot and covering it only after the water has come to a full boil. The broccoli will not, however, keep its brilliant green color after cooking unless it is refreshed by being run under cold water.

A NOTE ON THE RECIPES

This is not a diet cookbook by any means. However, one cannot disregard the importance of eating healthy, nutritious food with a minimum of fat, and I have attempted to develop recipes that reflect this thinking. For those who are on restricted diets or who wish, for one reason or another, to reduce their intake of fats and cholesterol, substitutions in the recipes may easily be made. For example:

Skim *or* low-fat milk for whole milk
Plain yogurt for sour cream
Canola oil, olive oil, *or* light olive oil for
butter *or* margarine

In addition, there are a number of reduced-fat products on the market that I find particularly good, such as reduced-calorie sour cream and lite mayonnaise. These substitutions may be made without drastically altering the taste of the recipes.

The most important consideration is that these recipes meet not only your dietary needs but also your preferences for certain foods. Do not be afraid to substitute ingredients in order to take advantage of seasonal produce—and of your own creativity. Most important, have fun. Enjoy yourself, and your enjoyment will be reflected in the food you prepare. These recipes are meant to be guidelines. They work very well if prepared as given, but there's nothing to say they wouldn't be equally delicious structured to your own personal tastes.

SOUPS

CREAM OF BROCCOLI SOUP

This soup makes a lovely opener to an elegant dinner. Garnish with toasted herbed croutons or serve with warm dinner rolls or French bread. The soup may also be served as a lunch entrée, accompanied by crusty bread and a salad.

1 cup chopped leeks (white part only)
2 red-skinned potatoes, cubed
2 tablespoons vegetable oil
4 cups coarsely chopped broccoli

6 cups chicken stock or broth
Salt
Pepper
½ cup plain yogurt, sour cream, or heavy cream

In a large saucepan, cook the leeks and potatoes in the oil over moderate heat, covered, stirring occasionally, for 5 minutes. Add the broccoli, chicken stock, and salt and pepper to taste, and simmer, covered, for 30 minutes. Puree the soup in batches in a food processor, return to the saucepan, and stir in the yogurt. Warm over moderate heat, stirring, until hot. Makes 8 cups, serving 4 to 6.

CURRIED SPLIT-PEA SOUP WITH BROCCOLI

Curry powder provides the flavoring in this soup. If possible, buy imported curry powder, which tends to have a more mellow and sophisticated taste. If you don't like curry, simply eliminate: The soup is equally good without it. Serve with toasted pita bread as either a first course or as a lunch entrée.

1½ cups yellow split peas, soaked in cold water to cover for 2 hours

2 cups finely chopped yellow onion

½ cup diced celery

½ cup sliced carrots

2 tablespoons vegetable oil

2 to 3 cloves garlic, finely minced

2 tablespoons imported curry powder (or to taste)

1 bay leaf

8 cups chicken stock or broth

3 cups broccoli florets, cut into 1½" × ¼" pieces

Plain yogurt and minced coriander for garnish (optional)

In a large saucepan over moderate heat, cook the onion, celery, and carrots in the vegetable oil for 3 minutes, stirring occasionally. Add the garlic and curry powder, and continue to cook, stirring occasionally, for 1 minute. Add the drained split peas, bay leaf, and chicken stock. Simmer, stirring and skimming occasionally, for 30 minutes, or until the peas are quite soft. Discard the bay leaf. Bring the soup to a boil, add the broccoli, and turn down the heat to a simmer. Stir for about 3 minutes, or until the broccoli is just tender. Serve garnished with yogurt and coriander, if desired. Makes 8 cups, serving 4 to 6.

BROCCOLI AND CHEDDAR CHEESE SOUP

The flavors of broccoli, Cheddar cheese, and red bell pepper blend beautifully in this hearty soup. If desired, crisp crumbled bacon may be added as garnish.

2 cups finely chopped yellow
   onion
2 cloves garlic, finely minced
3 tablespoons vegetable oil
1 large red-skinned potato, cubed
4 cups chicken stock or broth
1 bay leaf
Salt

Pepper
3 cups broccoli florets
1 medium red bell pepper, seeded
   and finely minced
3 tablespoons water
1 cup plain yogurt, sour cream, or
   low-fat milk
1 cup grated Cheddar cheese

In a large saucepan over moderate heat, cook the onion and garlic in 2 tablespoons of oil for 3 minutes, stirring occasionally. Add the potato, chicken stock, bay leaf, and salt and pepper to taste, and simmer, covered, stirring occasionally, for 20 minutes, or until the potato is tender. Discard the bay leaf. Puree the soup in batches in a food processor, return it to the saucepan, and bring to a simmer.

Meanwhile, in a 10-inch skillet over moderate heat, cook the broccoli and bell pepper in the remaining tablespoon of oil, stirring, for 1 minute. Add the 3 tablespoons of water, cover, and steam over moderately high heat for 2 minutes.

Remove the pureed soup mixture from the heat and stir in the yogurt. Gradually add the cheese, stirring until melted. Stir in the broccoli and red pepper and bring the soup to a simmer, stirring. Makes 8 cups, serving 4 to 6.

JAPANESE MISO SOUP WITH BROCCOLI

This is a wonderfully light and refreshing soup, ideal for warm weather. It can serve as the perfect prelude to a sumptuous dinner.

1 medium yellow onion, finely chopped
2 cloves garlic, finely minced
1 tablespoon minced fresh ginger-root
2 tablespoons vegetable oil
1 cup sliced carrots
6 cups chicken stock or broth
1 tablespoon miso (soybean paste), available at Oriental and specialty food markets

Salt
Pepper
3 cups blanched and refreshed broccoli florets (p. 86)
½ pound firm-textured bean curd, rinsed and cut into ½-inch cubes

In a large saucepan over moderate heat, cook the onion, garlic, and gingerroot in the oil, stirring, for 3 minutes. Add the carrots and toss for 1 minute. Stir in the chicken stock, miso, and salt and pepper to taste, and simmer, covered, for 20 minutes. Add the broccoli and bean curd and cook at a bare simmer for 5 minutes, or until the broccoli is just heated through. Makes 8 cups, serving 4 to 6.

SALADS

BROCCOLI AND TORTELLINI SALAD PRIMAVERA

Any small filled pasta will do—tortellini, cappelletti, or raviolini. Let the season dictate your choice of vegetables—just try to have a colorful mix and different textures.

½ pound cheese- or meat-filled
    tortellini
3 cups broccoli florets
1 medium yellow squash (½
    pound), halved lengthwise and
    sliced
1 cup diced tomatoes
½ cup drained and finely chopped
    olive-oil-packed sun-dried
    tomatoes

½ cup minced red onion
¼ cup minced fresh basil, chives,
    tarragon, or parsley (or try a
    combination)
6 tablespoons extra-virgin olive oil
2 tablespoons balsamic vinegar
Salt
Pepper
⅓ cup toasted pine nuts

Cook the pasta in a large pot of lightly salted boiling water for 5 minutes, stirring occasionally. Add the broccoli and boil for 2 minutes. Add the yellow squash and continue boiling for another minute. Drain the pasta and vegetables, refresh under cold water, and pat dry.

Transfer the pasta and vegetables to a large serving dish and add the two kinds of tomatoes, red onion, and herbs. Sprinkle with the olive oil, vinegar, and salt and pepper to taste, and toss to combine well. Garnish with pine nuts. Serves 4.

BROCCOLI-BROWN RICE SALAD

The citrus dressing in this salad enhances the flavors of the vegetables and dried fruits. However, a simple mixture of olive oil and vinegar or lemon juice, along with a touch of nut oil, may be substituted if desired.

4 cups cooked brown rice
2 cups blanched broccoli florets
  (p. 86)
½ cup minced red onion
½ cup mixed dried fruit (diced
  apricots, black or yellow raisins)
½ cup diced celery
½ cup coarsely chopped toasted
  walnuts

FOR THE DRESSING:
¼ cup fresh orange juice
1 tablespoon fresh lemon juice
1 tablespoon balsamic vinegar
2 teaspoons minced fresh gingerroot
½ teaspoon grated orange peel
Salt
Pepper
5 tablespoons vegetable oil
1 tablespoon walnut oil (optional)

In a large serving dish, combine the rice, broccoli, onion, dried fruit, celery, and walnuts. In a bowl, whisk together the orange juice, lemon juice, vinegar, ginger-root, and orange peel. Add salt and pepper to taste. Add the oil in a stream, whisking, and toss the salad with the dressing. Serves 6.

PANZANELLA (ITALIAN BREAD SALAD) WITH BROCCOLI

. . . .

An ingenious and quite delicious way to use leftover bread.

3 cups cubed and toasted stale white or *whole-grain French or Italian bread*
2 cups blanched broccoli florets (p. 86)
1 medium red bell pepper, diced
1 cup halved ripe cherry tomatoes
½ cup minced scallions
1 cup diced, peeled, and seeded cucumber

½ cup pitted black olives
⅓ cup minced fresh basil
2 tablespoons balsamic vinegar
1 to 2 cloves finely minced garlic
Salt
Pepper
6 tablespoons extra-virgin olive oil

In a large bowl, combine the bread cubes, broccoli, pepper, tomatoes, scallions, cucumber, olives, and basil. In a small bowl, whisk the vinegar, garlic, and salt and pepper to taste. Add the oil in a stream, whisking until dressing is well combined. Add to the salad and toss. Chill, covered, for at least 1 hour. Serves 4 to 6.

INDONESIAN VEGETABLE SALAD
WITH PEANUT SAUCE

As with the Salad Primavera (p. 17), the vegetables here may vary according to the seasons. Rinsed and blanched bean sprouts make a lovely addition and lend a fine Oriental flavor to this dish.

2 cups blanched broccoli florets
   (p. 86)
1 cup cooked sliced carrots
1 cup blanched and refreshed snow
   peas
1 cup cooked sliced potatoes
2 plum tomatoes, cut into wedges
1 6-inch piece of seedless European
   cucumber, sliced
1 3-inch square firm-textured bean
   curd, cut into ½-inch cubes

FOR THE SAUCE:
½ cup chicken stock or broth
½ cup smooth peanut butter
2 tablespoons lite soy sauce
2 tablespoons Oriental sesame oil
1 tablespoon finely minced garlic
1 tablespoon rice or cider vinegar
¼ teaspoon red pepper flakes

Arrange the broccoli, carrots, snow peas, potatoes, tomatoes, cucumber, and bean curd on a large serving dish. In a food processor or blender, combine all the sauce ingredients and puree until smooth. Serve the sauce with the salad. Serves 4 to 6.

THE BIG BROCCOLI BOOK

BULGUR (CRACKED WHEAT) SALAD WITH BROCCOLI AND TOMATOES

This is a wonderfully refreshing salad, particularly with the addition of fresh mint. Serve in summer with grilled meats and fish.

1 cup bulgur
2 cups boiling water
⅓ cup olive oil
3 tablespoons fresh lemon juice
1 tablespoon minced garlic
Salt
Pepper
2 cups blanched broccoli florets
   (p. 86)

2 medium-sized ripe tomatoes,
   cored, seeded, and chopped
1 small green bell pepper, seeded
   and diced
1 cup minced scallions
½ cup minced fresh parsley leaves
¼ cup minced fresh mint (optional)

Put the bulgur in a large heatproof bowl and pour the boiling water over it. Cover and let stand for 30 minutes. Drain and squeeze dry. In a small bowl, combine the olive oil, lemon juice, and garlic. Add salt and pepper to taste.

Combine the bulgur with the remaining vegetables in a large serving dish, and toss with the dressing. Serves 6.

CRISP GARDEN SALAD

. . . .

Choose the freshest vegetables for this pure and simple salad. Serve it well chilled.

2 cups broccoli florets
1 cup sliced carrots
1 red bell pepper, seeded and cut
    into strips
½ cup minced scallions

FOR THE DRESSING:
⅓ cup mayonnaise

⅓ cup plain yogurt or sour cream
1 tablespoon cider vinegar
2 teaspoons Dijon mustard
Pinch of sugar
2 tablespoons minced fresh dill,
    basil, or parsley
Salt
Pepper

In a serving bowl, combine the broccoli, carrots, red pepper, and scallions. In a small bowl, mix together the mayonnaise, yogurt, vinegar, mustard, sugar, dill, and salt and pepper to taste. Add the dressing to the salad and toss it gently to coat the vegetables. Cover and chill until ready to serve. Serves 4.

SEAFOOD

BROCCOLI STIR-FRY WITH SHRIMP AND GINGERROOT

You can also prepare this stir-fry with scallops or other shellfish and serve with brown rice or noodles.

3 tablespoons vegetable oil
1 pound large shrimp, shelled and deveined
Salt
1 tablespoon minced fresh gingerroot
2 tablespoons minced scallions
2 cloves garlic, minced
3 cups broccoli florets

1 cup (1 8-ounce can) sliced water chestnuts
4 tablespoons chicken stock or broth
2 tablespoons dry sherry
2 tablespoons lite soy sauce
¼ teaspoon red pepper flakes
1 tablespoon Oriental sesame oil

In a wok or 12-inch nonstick skillet, heat 1 tablespoon of oil until hot. Add the shrimp and salt to taste and stir-fry over moderately high heat for 1 to 2 minutes, or until the shrimp is pink and opaque. Transfer the shrimp to a plate. Add the remaining oil to the wok. When hot, add the gingerroot, scallions, and garlic, and stir-fry for 30 seconds. Add the broccoli and water chestnuts, and stir-fry for 1 minute. Add the broth, sherry, soy sauce, and red pepper flakes, cover, and steam for 2 minutes. Return the shrimp to the wok and stir-fry for 1 minute, or until heated through. Swirl in the sesame oil and transfer to a heated serving dish. Serves 4.

BROCCOLI AND CRAB SOUFFLÉ

. . . .

Substitute cooked shrimp or scallops for the crab, if desired. Or simply eliminate the fish altogether and increase the amount of broccoli by 1 cup.

FOR THE BASE:

3 tablespoons unsalted butter or margarine

¼ cup all-purpose flour

1½ cups milk, scalded

Cayenne and freshly grated nutmeg to taste

Salt

4 large egg yolks

2 teaspoons Dijon mustard

½ cup grated cheese, such as Gruyère or Cheddar

FOR THE FILLING:

½ cup minced shallots or onion

2 cloves garlic, finely minced

2 tablespoons unsalted butter

2 cups blanched (p. 86) and chopped broccoli

1 cup flaked crabmeat

5 large egg whites

2 tablespoons freshly grated Parmesan

Preheat oven to 400°.

MAKE THE BASE: In a medium-heavy saucepan, melt the butter, add the flour, and whisk over moderately low heat for 3 minutes. Add the milk, bring the mixture back to a simmer, whisking, and season with the cayenne, nutmeg, and salt to taste. Simmer the sauce over moderately low heat, stirring occasionally until it thickens, about 5 minutes. Remove from heat and beat in the egg yolks, one at a time. Add the Dijon mustard and the grated Gruyère or Cheddar.

MAKE THE FILLING: In a 10-inch skillet, cook the shallots and garlic in the butter over moderate heat, stirring, for 2 minutes. Add the broccoli and crabmeat and cook, stirring occasionally, for 3 minutes. Fold the filling into the soufflé base.

In a large bowl, with an electric mixer, beat the whites until they hold stiff but not dry peaks. Stir ¼ of the egg whites into the soufflé base and fold in the remaining whites gently but thoroughly. Transfer the mixture to a buttered 6-cup soufflé dish and sprinkle with the Parmesan. Put the souffle in the oven. Reduce the heat to 375° and bake for 30 to 35 minutes, or until it is puffed and golden brown. Serves 4.

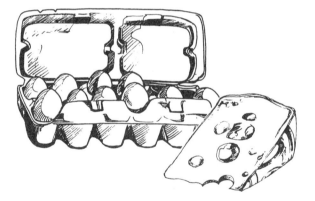

BROCCOLI WITH TUNA AND CANNELLINI BEANS

Serve this entrée for lunch accompanied by warm crusty rolls and a side dish of firm-ripe tomatoes with fresh basil, if in season.

1 10-ounce can cannellini beans, drained and rinsed thoroughly

1 6½-ounce can solid white-meat tuna, flaked

½ cup minced red onion

1 clove garlic, finely minced

2 tablespoons minced fresh parsley

½ pound broccoli, separated into 2-inch florets, stalks peeled and cut into 1" × ¼" lengths

3 tablespoons extra-virgin olive oil

2 tablespoons lemon juice

Salt

Pepper

In a serving bowl, combine the beans, tuna, onion, garlic, and parsley.

In a 10-inch nonstick skillet, combine the broccoli with ¼ cup water, bring to a boil over moderately high heat, cover, and steam for 2 to 3 minutes, or until crisp tender. If necessary, pour off any water remaining in the pan and transfer the broccoli to the serving bowl. Sprinkle with the olive oil, lemon juice, and salt and pepper to taste. Fold gently until combined. Serves 4.

BROCCOLI AND SHRIMP-STUFFED POTATOES

Twice-baked potatoes have always been a favorite around our house. They are particularly well suited to advance preparation and therefore make a wonderfully quick and informal party dish.

2 large Idaho or russet baking
   potatoes
2 tablespoons vegetable oil
1 onion, minced
2 cloves garlic, minced
2 cups 1-inch pieces of broccoli
¼ cup water
1 cup diced cooked shrimp

½ cup sour cream or plain yogurt
Salt
Pepper
3 tablespoons freshly grated Parmesan cheese
1 tablespoon unsalted butter or margarine, cut into bits

Preheat oven to 400°.

Wash the potatoes, prick them, and bake in a preheated oven for 1 hour or until tender. Set aside until cool enough to handle.

In a 10-inch nonstick skillet, heat the oil over moderate heat. Add the onion and cook for 5 to 7 minutes, stirring occasionally, until it is golden. Add the garlic and broccoli, and cook, stirring, for 1 minute. Add ¼ cup water, cover, and let steam for 2 to 3 minutes, or until crisp tender. If necessary, pour off any remaining water from the pan.

Halve the potatoes lengthwise. Scoop the flesh into a bowl, leaving a thin shell.

Mash the scooped-out potato. Add the broccoli mixture, shrimp, sour cream, and salt and pepper to taste. Stir gently until mixture is combined. Spoon the filling into the potato shells and transfer them to a well-buttered shallow baking dish. Spoon any leftover filling around the potato shells. Sprinkle the top of the potatoes with the Parmesan and dot with the butter or margarine. Bake in the oven for 15 to 20 minutes, until heated through. Serves 2.

BROCCOLI AND SEAFOOD CREPES

This is a wonderful dish to serve at parties. It may be completely prepared and assembled a day ahead of time, and can be served directly from the baking dish. Cooked chicken may be substituted for the seafood if desired. Whichever you choose, accompany the crepes with a crisp green salad.

1 recipe Basic Crepe Batter (p. 34)
6 tablespoons unsalted butter or
   margarine
1 cup minced onion
2 cloves garlic, minced
3 cups 1-inch pieces of broccoli
½ cup chicken stock or broth
Salt
Pepper

4 tablespoons all-purpose flour
2½ cups milk
Freshly grated nutmeg to taste
1 cup grated cheese (Cheddar,
   Swiss, or Monterey Jack)
2 cups cooked diced shrimp, crab,
   or lobster
2 tablespoons freshly grated
   Parmesan cheese

Prepare the crepe batter according to the instructions on p. 34. Let stand for one hour.

Melt 2 tablespoons of the butter in a large skillet over moderate heat. Add the onion and garlic, and cook, stirring, for 3 minutes, or until softened. Add the broccoli, chicken broth, and salt and pepper to taste. Bring the liquid to a boil, cover, and steam for 3 minutes, or until tender. Transfer the mixture to a bowl.

Melt the remaining butter in a saucepan, add the flour, and cook over low heat, stirring, for 3 minutes. Add the milk, freshly grated nutmeg, and add salt and pepper to taste. Bring to a boil and simmer, stirring occasionally, for 5 minutes. Remove from heat and stir in the cheese. Add 1 cup of the sauce to the broccoli mixture along with the seafood and combine well.

MAKE THE CREPES: Preheat oven to 350°. Spoon ¼ cup of the filling down the center of each crepe, fold the sides over, and turn into a buttered shallow baking dish, seam side down. Spoon the remaining cheese sauce over the crepes. Sprinkle with the Parmesan.

Bake in the oven for 30 to 40 minutes, or until the sauce is bubbling. Serves 6.

BASIC CREPE BATTER

· ·

3 large eggs

1 cup milk

3 tablespoons unsalted butter or
   margarine, melted

¼ teaspoon salt

1 cup all-purpose flour

Melted butter or margarine for
   cooking the crepes

Combine all the ingredients in a blender or food processor and blend until smooth. Transfer to a bowl, cover loosely, and let stand 1 hour.

Heat a 7-inch crepe pan or skillet over moderately high heat. Brush the pan with melted butter and pour a scant ¼ cup batter into the pan. Quickly tip the pan back and forth so that the batter coats the bottom evenly. Cook for about 1 minute over moderate heat or until the edges are golden brown. Slide a spatula under the crepe, flip it over, and cook for about 30 seconds longer. Transfer to a plate. Continue until all the remaining batter is used.

The crepes may be cooled to room temperature, separated by sheets of wax paper, then covered with plastic wrap and refrigerated for up to 24 hours. They can also be frozen. Makes about 10 crepes.

POULTRY

BROCCOLI AND CHICKEN TACOS

. . . .

These tacos make a nutritious informal lunch for your guests or children. You'll be amazed at how delicious they are. Cooked canned beans, such as kidney beans or cannellini beans, drained and rinsed, may be substituted for the chicken if desired.

1½ cups finely chopped onion
1 cup diced green bell pepper
2 tablespoons vegetable oil
2 cloves garlic, finely minced
1 tablespoon chili powder
2 teaspoons ground cumin
1 14-ounce can whole tomatoes,
    pureed with their liquid
1 tablespoon tomato paste
2 cups blanched broccoli (p. 86),
    chopped

2 cups diced cooked chicken
Salt
Pepper
2 tablespoons minced fresh ci-
    lantro
12 taco shells (1 package)

FOR THE TOPPINGS:
Serve shredded cheese, shredded
    lettuce, sour cream, guacamole,
    and taco salsa

Preheat oven to 350°.

In a medium saucepan over moderate heat, cook the onion and pepper in the oil, stirring occasionally, for 5 minutes. Add the garlic, chili powder, and cumin, and cook, stirring, for 1 minute. Add the tomato puree and the tomato paste, and simmer, stirring occasionally, for 5 minutes. Stir in the broccoli, chicken, and salt and pepper to taste, and continue to simmer, stirring occasionally, until the vegetables are just heated through. Mix in the cilantro.

Warm the taco shells in the oven for 7 to 10 minutes. Spoon the filling into the shells and serve hot with the toppings. Serves 6.

BROCCOLI, CHICKEN, AND CHILI CHEESE GRATIN

Prepare this dish when you have leftover chicken or seafood. It makes a delicious "Southwestern" hors d'oeuvre, served with taco chips or toasted pita triangles.

2 cups blanched broccoli (p. 86) chopped

2 cups diced cooked chicken

½ cup mayonnaise

1 cup grated Monterey Jack or Cheddar cheese

⅓ cup grated Parmesan cheese

2 teaspoons ground cumin

1 4-ounce can chilies, drained and chopped

1 cup peeled, seeded, and chopped tomatoes, or 1 14-ounce can tomatoes, drained and chopped

2 tablespoons minced fresh cilantro

Salt

Pepper

1 tablespoon unsalted butter or margarine

Preheat oven to 400°.

In a large bowl, combine the broccoli, chicken, mayonnaise, Monterey Jack or Cheddar cheese, all but 2 tablespoons of the Parmesan, the cumin, chilies, tomatoes, cilantro, and salt and pepper to taste. Transfer the mixture to a buttered baking dish, sprinkle with the remaining Parmesan, and dot with the butter. Bake in the oven for 20 to 25 minutes. Serves 6 to 8 as an hors d'oeuvre.

CURRIED CHICKEN WITH BROCCOLI AND SHIITAKE MUSHROOMS

. . . .

Add plain rice, or a saffron- or brown-rice pilaf, and a crisp salad, and you have a simple, fast, unexpected-guest dish. Warmed pita bread makes a nice accompaniment.

3 tablespoons vegetable or canola oil

4 boneless chicken breast halves (about 1½ pounds), rinsed and patted dry

Salt

Pepper

1 onion, minced

1 red bell pepper, seeded and minced

1 tablespoon imported curry powder

2 tablespoons all-purpose flour

1½ cups chicken stock or broth

1 bay leaf

¼ pound fresh shiitake or white mushrooms

1 clove garlic, minced

2 cups broccoli florets

¼ cup water

½ cup plain yogurt

Minced fresh cilantro and toasted sliced almonds for garnish (optional)

In a 12-inch nonstick skillet, heat 2 tablespoons of the oil over moderate heat. When hot, add the chicken breasts, and salt, and pepper to taste. Cook for 1 minute on each side, or until no longer pink. Transfer the chicken to a plate and set aside. Add the onion and red pepper to the skillet, and cook, stirring occasionally, for 5 minutes. Add the curry powder and flour, and cook over low heat, stirring, for 2 minutes. Add the chicken stock and bay leaf, bring to a simmer, stirring, and return the chicken to the pan. Simmer for another 10 minutes, or until the chicken is firm but still springy to the touch.

While the chicken is cooking, heat the remaining oil in a 10-inch nonstick skillet. Add the mushrooms, and cook, stirring, for 2 minutes. Add the garlic and broccoli, and cook, stirring, for 1 minute more. Pour in ¼ cup water, cover, and steam for 3 minutes or until crisp tender. Uncover and pour off any liquid remaining in the pan.

Stir the yogurt into the chicken until well combined and add the broccoli-mushroom mixture. Simmer uncovered over moderately low heat, stirring occasionally, for 3 to 4 minutes, or until heated through. Garnish with the cilantro and toasted almonds, if desired. Serves 4.

CHICKEN DIVAN

· · · · · · · · · · · · · · · · · · · ·

Some recipes withstand the test of time, becoming classics. This is one of them. An elegant way to use leftover chicken or turkey.

2 tablespoons unsalted butter or margarine
2 tablespoons all-purpose flour
1 cup chicken stock or broth
Freshly grated nutmeg
Salt
Pepper
½ cup heavy cream or half-and-half

¼ cup freshly grated Parmesan cheese
1 tablespoon dry sherry (optional)
½ pound broccoli, cut into pieces about 4 inches long, blanched and drained (p. 86)
6 slices cooked chicken

Preheat oven to 350°.

In a medium saucepan, melt the butter over moderately low heat, add the flour, and cook, stirring, for 2 minutes. Add the chicken stock, nutmeg, and salt and pepper to taste. Simmer 3 minutes, then stir in the cream, 2 tablespoons of the Parmesan, and the sherry if desired.

Arrange the broccoli and chicken in a buttered shallow baking dish (1-quart size), spoon the sauce over it, and sprinkle with the remaining cheese. Bake in the oven for 20 to 30 minutes. Serves 4.

TURKEY CUTLETS WITH BROCCOLI IN DILLED MUSTARD CREAM

The mustard cream sauce in this recipe blends beautifully with the flavors of broccoli and turkey. If fresh dill is not available, substitute fresh chives, fresh tarragon leaves, or fresh parsley.

4 turkey cutlets (about 1 pound),
 rinsed and patted dry
¼ cup all-purpose flour
3 tablespoons vegetable oil, unsalted butter, or margarine
Salt
Pepper
¼ cup minced shallots
1 clove garlic, minced
⅓ cup dry white wine

1 cup chicken stock or broth
½ teaspoon dried rosemary, crumbled
3 cups blanched broccoli florets
 (p.86)
½ cup sour cream or plain yogurt
2 teaspoons Dijon mustard
1 teaspoon cornstarch
2 tablespoons minced fresh dill

Dredge the turkey in the flour, shaking off the excess. In a 12-inch nonstick skillet, heat 2 tablespoons of the vegetable oil over moderately high heat. Add the turkey and salt and pepper to taste, and cook for 30 seconds on each side, or until it is no longer pink. Transfer the turkey to a large plate and set aside. Add the remaining oil or butter to the skillet, and heat. Add the shallots and garlic, and cook, stirring occasionally, for 3 minutes. Add the wine and reduce it for 1 minute over moderately high heat. Add the chicken stock, rosemary, the reserved turkey, and the broccoli to the skillet. Bring the liquid to a boil and simmer, covered, for 2 to 3 minutes, or until heated through. Remove the turkey and broccoli from the liquid, place on a serving dish, and keep warm, covered loosely.

In a small bowl, whisk together the sour cream, mustard, and cornstarch. Return the liquid in the skillet to a simmer and stir in the sour-cream mixture. Simmer, stirring, for 2 minutes. Correct seasoning, adding more salt and pepper to taste, and stir in the dill. Spoon the sauce over the turkey and broccoli. Serves 4.

MEAT

· · · · · · · · · · · · · · · · · · · ·

BROCCOLI STIR-FRIED BEEF WITH GINGER AND DRIED MUSHROOMS

. . . .

A favorite and easy combination.

1 ounce dried shiitake mushrooms,
    about 4 large
1 cup boiling water
1 tablespoon dry sherry
2 tablespoons lite soy sauce
2 tablespoons vegetable oil
1 tablespoon minced fresh ginger-
    root
1 tablespoon minced garlic

1 pound sirloin, cut into thin strips
2 scallions, minced
3 cups broccoli florets, cut into
    2-inch lengths
2 teaspoons cornstarch, dissolved
    in 1 tablespoon water
1 to 2 tablespoons Oriental sesame
    oil, or to taste

Soak the mushrooms in the water for 30 minutes. Drain, reserving ½ cup of the liquid. Remove stems and cut into slices. In a small bowl, combine the soaking liquid with the sherry and soy sauce.

In a wok or 12-inch nonstick skillet, heat 1 tablespoon of the oil over moderately high heat. Add the gingerroot and garlic, and stir-fry for 30 seconds. Add the beef and mushrooms, and stir-fry until the beef loses its pink color—about 3 minutes. Transfer the mixture to a plate and set aside.

Add the remaining oil to the skillet and stir-fry the scallions for 30 seconds. Add the broccoli and stir-fry for 2 minutes. Stir in the beef mixture and mushroom-soaking liquid, and steam, covered, for 1 minute. Whisk the cornstarch mixture, add it to the skillet, and cook, stirring, until the sauce thickens slightly. Swirl in the sesame oil and transfer to a serving plate. Serves 4.

THE BIG BROCCOLI BOOK

LAMB AND BROCCOLI COUSCOUS

Couscous is the national dish of Morocco, Algeria, and Tunisia. It is a festive dish that is admirably suited to large parties. Classically, it is served with harissa, a fiery condiment made from ground chilies and a combination of exotic spices. Many specialty food stores carry this already made, but use it sparingly—it's dynamite!

1½ pounds boneless lamb shoulder, cut into 1½-inch pieces
Salt
Pepper
2 tablespoons vegetable oil
2 cups chopped onion
2 cloves garlic, finely minced
1 16-ounce can tomatoes, including liquid, chopped
2 teaspoons ground cumin
1 teaspoon dried thyme, crumbled
½ teaspoon ground ginger

1 cinnamon stick
4 cups beef stock or broth
1 cup thickly sliced carrots
2 cups blanched broccoli florets (p. 86)
1 medium yellow squash, cut into 1-inch pieces
1 10½-ounce can chick-peas, drained
2 cups couscous, cooked according to package directions
Harissa (optional)

Pat the lamb dry and season it with salt and pepper. Heat the oil in a large casserole over moderately high heat, add the lamb, and brown on all sides. Transfer to a plate and set aside. Add the onions to the casserole and cook, stirring occasionally, until they are a pale golden brown—about 5 minutes. Add the garlic, tomatoes, cumin, thyme, ginger, cinnamon, beef stock, and the reserved lamb. Bring the liquid to a boil, skimming, then turn down heat and simmer, covered, for 1 to 1½ hours, or until the lamb is tender. Add the carrots and simmer, covered, for 8 minutes. Stir in the broccoli, the squash, and the chick-peas, and simmer, covered, for 5 minutes more, or until the vegetables are just tender. Remove the cinnamon stick, and serve the lamb and vegetables with the couscous. Accompany with the harissa, if desired. Serves 6.

THE BIG BROCCOLI BOOK

BROCCOLI, HAM, AND CHEESE BREAD PUDDING

Perfect for a festive breakfast or brunch, this dish may be prepared up to one day ahead. As an alternative to the ham, try cooked Italian sausage meat.

2 tablespoons vegetable oil

1 onion, minced

3 cups broccoli florets, cut into 1-inch pieces, along with the stalks, peeled and cubed

¼ cup water

1 7-ounce jar pimentos, drained and chopped

Salt

Pepper

4 large eggs

1½ cups milk

2 teaspoons Dijon mustard

Cayenne

4½ cups 1-inch bread cubes (whole-grain or white bread may be used, but if using whole-wheat, be sure it is not too sweet)

1 cup diced cooked ham

2 cups grated Monterey Jack or Cheddar cheese

In a 10-inch nonstick skillet, heat the oil over moderate heat. Add the onion and cook, stirring occasionally, for 3 minutes. Add the broccoli and ¼ cup water; cover and steam over moderately high heat for 2 to 3 minutes, or until crisp tender. Add the pimentos, and salt and pepper to taste. Stir 1 to 2 minutes or until mixture is dry.

In a bowl, whisk together the eggs, milk, mustard, cayenne, and salt and pepper to taste. Arrange half the bread cubes in a 13″ × 9″ × 2″ buttered shallow baking dish, cover with half the broccoli and half the ham, and pour half the egg mixture over all. Add half the grated cheese, the remaining bread, broccoli, ham, egg mixture, and remaining cheese in layers, and let the pudding stand, covered with buttered foil, for at least 1 hour, or chill overnight.

Preheat oven to 400°.

Bake the still-covered pudding for 15 minutes. Uncover, and bake 10 or 15 minutes longer, or until bubbling. (If the pudding is chilled, add 10 to 12 minutes to the cooking time.) Serves 6.

BEEF AND BROCCOLI ENCHILADAS

Always a hit with young and old alike. Easy to make and assemble, these enchiladas may be prepared up to one day in advance.

1 cup minced onion
½ cup diced and seeded green bell
  pepper
2 tablespoons vegetable oil
2 cloves garlic, minced
½ pound ground beef or a combination of beef and pork
2 teaspoons chili powder
2 teaspoons ground cumin
Salt
Pepper
1½ cups canned crushed tomatoes
  in puree

½ teaspoon dried oregano, crumbled
½ teaspoon thyme, crumbled
2 cups blanched broccoli (p. 86),
  diced
1½ cups grated Monterey Jack or
  Cheddar cheese
6 7-inch flour tortillas, heated
  according to package directions
1 8-ounce jar enchilada or taco
  sauce

Preheat oven to 400°.

TO MAKE THE SAUCE: In a skillet, cook the onion and green pepper in the oil over moderate heat, stirring occasionally, for 5 minutes. Add the garlic, beef, chili powder, cumin, and salt and pepper to taste. Continue stirring until the beef loses its pink color. Add the tomatoes, oregano, and thyme, and simmer, stirring occasionally, for 20 minutes. Remove from heat and set aside 1 cup of the sauce.

ASSEMBLE THE ENCHILADAS: Arrange a tortilla on your work surface, add a line of broccoli down the center, spoon some of the sauce over it, and sprinkle with cheese. (Reserve ½ cup of cheese for the topping.) Fold the sides of the tortillas up over the filling and transfer the enchiladas, seam side down, to an oiled shallow baking dish. Continue until all the tortillas are used up. In a bowl, combine the remaining cup of meat sauce with the enchilada sauce, and spoon over the tortillas. Sprinkle with the remaining ½ cup of cheese, cover with foil, and bake in the oven for 20 minutes, or until heated through. Serves 6.

GRAINS
AND PASTA
· ·

RISOTTO WITH BROCCOLI

The time taken to make risotto is worth every minute. The creamy texture of a well-prepared risotto blends beautifully with broccoli and cheese. This is comfort food at its best.

3 to 4 cups chicken stock or *broth*
3 tablespoons unsalted butter or *margarine*
1 cup minced onion
1 cup Arborio (Italian short-grain) or *long-grain rice*
Salt

Pepper
½ cup dry white wine
2 cups blanched broccoli florets, (p. 86)
3 tablespoons freshly grated Parmesan cheese

In a medium saucepan, heat the stock to a simmer and keep warm.

In a large, deep, heavy saucepan set over moderate heat, melt 2 tablespoons of the butter, add the onion, and cook for 3 minutes. Add the rice and salt and pepper, and stir for 2 minutes more. Pour in the wine and simmer the mixture, stirring, until all the wine is absorbed. Add ½ cup of the hot stock to the pan and simmer, stirring, until almost all the liquid is absorbed. Continue adding the stock, ½ cup at a time, stirring and simmering throughout. It is critical that each ½ cup of liquid is absorbed before the next is added. The rice should be al dente when finished. (Total cooking time is about 20 to 30 minutes.) Stir in the broccoli and cook until the mixture is heated through. Fold in the cheese and remaining butter and serve immediately. Serves 4.

BROCCOLI RICE WITH TOMATOES, CAPERS, AND OLIVES

. . . .

This rice is delicious with roast chicken, duck, or pork.

1 cup finely chopped onion
1 green bell pepper, diced
2 tablespoons olive oil
1 16-ounce can tomatoes, drained
  and chopped
1 tablespoon minced garlic
1½ cups long-grain rice
2½ cups chicken stock or broth
1 teaspoon dried thyme

¼ teaspoon saffron threads
1 bay leaf
2 cups blanched broccoli florets
  (p. 86)
Salt
Pepper
½ cup sliced pimento-stuffed
  olives
2 tablespoons drained capers

In a medium saucepan, cook the onion and pepper in the oil over moderate heat, stirring occasionally, for 3 minutes. Add the tomatoes and garlic, and cook the mixture, stirring, for 2 minutes. Add the rice, chicken stock, thyme, saffron, bay leaf, broccoli, and salt and pepper to taste; return to a simmer, stirring; cover, and cook for 18 to 20 minutes, or until rice is tender. Let stand for 5 minutes and stir in the olives and capers. Serves 4 to 6.

BROCCOLI AND BROWN RICE CASSEROLE

....

This dish is perfect entertainment fare, since it may be completely prepared ahead of time. Simply chill, covered, for several hours or overnight before baking. A combination of rices—brown, wild, and white—gives it an intriguing flavor.

3 tablespoons unsalted butter or
   margarine
1 small onion, finely minced
1 clove garlic, finely minced
2 tablespoons all-purpose flour
1 cup milk
1 cup sour cream or *plain yogurt*
2 teaspoons Dijon mustard
Salt

Pepper
3 cups cooked brown rice (or a
   combination of cooked brown,
   wild, and white rices)
3 cups blanched broccoli florets,
   (p. 86)
1 cup grated Monterey Jack or
   Cheddar cheese
Paprika

Preheat oven to 350°.

In a heavy saucepan, melt the butter over moderate heat, add the onion and garlic, and cook, stirring, for 2 minutes. Add the flour and stir over moderately low heat for 2 minutes more. Stir in the milk and simmer for 3 minutes. Add the sour cream, mustard, and salt and pepper to taste. In a large bowl, combine the sauce with the rice and broccoli and transfer to a buttered 1½-quart shallow baking dish. Sprinkle the top of the casserole with the cheese and dust with paprika. (Dish may be prepared ahead up to this point.)

Bake the casserole, covered with foil, in the oven for 30 minutes. Remove the foil and bake 10 minutes more, or until the cheese is melted. Serves 6.

THE BIG BROCCOLI BOOK

FUSILLI WITH BROCCOLI AND DRIED MUSHROOMS

. . . .

There are countless ways to prepare broccoli with pasta. This is one of the easiest and most pleasing.

½ ounce dried porcini or shiitake
   mushrooms
1 cup boiling water
⅓ cup olive oil
1 cup minced onion
2 cloves garlic, minced
½ teaspoon dried red pepper
   flakes

1 pound fusilli or similar pasta,
   cooked according to package directions and drained
4 cups blanched broccoli florets,
   (p. 86)
Salt
Pepper
Freshly grated Parmesan cheese

Soak the mushrooms in the water for 30 minutes. Drain, reserving the liquid, and slice, discarding the tough stems. Strain the soaking liquid through a fine sieve into a bowl, and set aside ½ cup.

In a large skillet, heat the oil over moderately high heat. When hot, add the onion, reduce heat to moderate, and cook, stirring occasionally, until it is lightly browned. Add the garlic and red pepper flakes, and cook, stirring, for 1 minute. Add the reserved mushroom liquid, pasta, broccoli, and salt and pepper to taste, and toss the mixture until it is heated through, about 2 to 3 minutes. Transfer to a large serving dish and sprinkle with the Parmesan. Serves 4 to 6.

BROCCOLI AND PASTA FRITTATA

· ·

Use leftover pasta to create this delicious spaghetti and broccoli "cake." Serve it hot, warm, or at room temperature.

1 cup sliced shallots or *onions*
4 tablespoons olive oil
2 cloves garlic, minced
1 1-pound can tomatoes, drained, seeded, and chopped (1 cup)
1 tablespoon tomato paste
1 tablespoon minced fresh basil
½ teaspoon dried oregano
4 large eggs
⅓ cup freshly grated Parmesan cheese

Salt
Pepper
3 cups (5 ounces dried) cooked pasta: spaghetti, linguine, or capellini
2 cups blanched broccoli florets (p. 86)
4 ounces mozzarella cheese, grated
Minced fresh herbs, such as basil, oregano, or *parsley*

Preheat the broiler.

In a large skillet, cook the shallots in 2 tablespoons of the oil over moderate heat, stirring occasionally, for 5 minutes or until golden. Add the garlic and cook, stirring, for 1 minute. Add the tomatoes, tomato paste, basil, oregano, and salt and pepper to taste. Simmer the mixture, stirring occasionally, until thick.

In a bowl, combine the eggs, all but 2 tablespoons of the Parmesan, and salt and pepper to taste.

In a 10-inch nonstick skillet, heat the remaining oil until hot, add the cooked pasta, and toss to coat well with the oil. Tap the pasta into an even layer, pour in the egg mixture, and cook over moderately low heat for 8 to 10 minutes, or until the bottom is golden brown when lifted slightly. Scatter the broccoli over the pasta, and top with the tomato mixture. Sprinkle with the mozzarella, remaining Parmesan, and fresh herbs. Put the frittata under the preheated broiler about 4 inches from the flame for 3 to 4 minutes, or until the cheese has melted. Slide onto a serving plate and cut into wedges. Serves 4 to 6.

BROCCOLI PILAF WITH CHICK-PEAS AND TOMATOES

· ·

This pilaf has a slightly East Indian flavor, and could well serve as an entrée, especially if accompanied by a fresh-tasting cucumber and yogurt salad with mint. Or serve it as a side dish with, among other things, shish kebab or marinated grilled beef.

2 tablespoons vegetable oil
1 cup chopped onion
2 or 3 cloves garlic, minced
2 teaspoons cumin seed
2 teaspoons minced fresh ginger-
    root or ¼ teaspoon ground
½ teaspoon dried thyme, crumbled
¼ teaspoon ground turmeric
1 1-pound can tomatoes, drained
    and chopped
2 cups Basmati (Indian long-grain
    rice) or plain long-grain rice

1 15-ounce can chick-peas, drained
    and rinsed
Salt
Pepper
3½ cups chicken stock or broth
2 cups blanched broccoli (p. 86), in
    ½-inch pieces
Minced fresh cilantro to taste
Lemon slices for garnish

Preheat oven to 350°.

In a medium-large casserole, heat the oil. When hot, add the onion, and cook, stirring occasionally, for 5 minutes, or until golden. Add the garlic, cumin, gingerroot, thyme, and turmeric. Cook, stirring, for 1 minute. Add the tomatoes and continue to cook, stirring, until the mixture is dry. Add the rice, chick-peas, and salt and pepper to taste. Stir until well combined, then add the chicken stock and the broccoli. Bring the mixture to a simmer. Place a round of wax paper over the top, and cover with the lid. Bake in the oven for 20 to 25 minutes, or until the rice is tender. Let stand for 5 minutes, then transfer to a serving dish and garnish with the cilantro and lemon slices. Serves 4 as an entrée and 6 to 8 as a side dish.

CAPELLINI WITH BROCCOLI AND FRESH TOMATO SAUCE

. . . .

Make this uncooked tomato sauce during the summer and early fall, when the fruit is at its peak and fresh herbs are plentiful.

2 cups peeled, seeded, and chopped
   tomatoes
½ cup extra-virgin olive oil
2 to 3 teaspoons minced garlic
½ cup firmly packed chopped fresh
   basil leaves

1 pound capellini or *similar pasta*
3 cups broccoli florets
Freshly grated Parmesan cheese

In a bowl, combine the tomatoes, oil, garlic, and basil and let sit at room temperature for 30 minutes.

Cook the capellini in a kettle of boiling salted water for 5 to 6 minutes; it should be very al dente. Add the broccoli and cook, stirring occasionally, for 3 to 4 minutes, or until the broccoli is tender. Drain and transfer to a large bowl. Add the sauce and toss the pasta and broccoli until it is well coated. Serve the pasta with the grated Parmesan. Serves 4 to 6.

MEATLESS ENTRÉES

BROCCOLI AND CHEESE QUICHE

. . . .

Packaged frozen pie shells work quite well here. The quiche may also be prepared without a shell. Simply butter your pie pan thoroughly and allow 5 to 10 minutes less cooking time.

1 ½ cups blanched broccoli (p. 86),
    chopped
1 9-inch prebaked pie shell
3 large eggs
1 cup milk, half-and-half,
    or *cream*

½ cup grated Gruyère or *Parmesan*
    cheese
Salt
Cayenne to taste

Preheat oven to 375°.

Sprinkle the broccoli over the bottom of the pie shell. In a bowl, whisk together the eggs, milk, cheese, salt, and cayenne to taste. Pour the custard into the pie shell and bake on a baking sheet in the oven for 35 to 40 minutes, or until puffed and golden. Serves 4 to 6.

POTATO-BROCCOLI RICOTTA PIE

The next time you have leftover mashed potatoes, think of this pie. It's a slightly different way to serve broccoli and potatoes—an all-in-one elegant dish.

1 9-inch prebaked pie shell
2 cups blanched broccoli (p. 86),
    chopped
2 cups mashed potatoes
1 cup part-skim ricotta cheese
½ cup plain yogurt or sour cream
½ cup sliced scallions

2 large eggs
1 teaspoon salt
¼ teaspoon pepper
¼ cup freshly grated Parmesan
    cheese
Paprika

Preheat oven to 350°.

Place the pie shell on a baking sheet. In a bowl, combine the broccoli, potatoes, ricotta, yogurt, scallions, eggs, salt, and pepper. Gently stir the mixture until it is thoroughly combined. Pour the filling into the pie shell, smoothing the top, and sprinkle it with the Parmesan. Add paprika to taste. Bake in the oven for 60 minutes, or until golden brown. Serves 4 to 6.

SAUTÉED BROCCOLI AND CHERRY TOMATOES

Arrange this colorful combination of broccoli and cherry tomatoes in the shape of a Christmas wreath to add a festive look to your holiday table.

*1 bunch of broccoli (about 1½
    pounds), separated into 2-inch
    florets, stalks peeled and cut into
    1½-inch sticks, blanched (p. 86)*
1 pint cherry tomatoes
3 tablespoons olive oil

Salt
Pepper
1 clove garlic, finely minced
*2 tablespoons minced fresh chives,
    tarragon, or dill*

Pat dry the broccoli.

In a 12-inch nonstick skillet, cook the cherry tomatoes in the oil with salt and pepper to taste, stirring, over moderate heat, for 1 minute. Add the garlic and the broccoli. Taste and add more salt and pepper if needed. Cook, stirring occasionally, over moderate heat for 3 to 4 minutes, or until the broccoli is heated through. Sprinkle with the fresh herbs. Serves 6.

BROCCOLI PIZZA WITH SMOKED MOZZARELLA AND SUN-DRIED TOMATOES

. . . .

Homemade pizza dough is a cinch if prepared in a food processor. However, if you don't have the time it takes for the dough to rise, simply buy ready-made pizza dough and proceed with the recipe for the topping.

FOR THE DOUGH:
1 package active dry yeast
¾ cup warm water
2 to 2¼ cups all-purpose flour
1 teaspoon salt
2 tablespoons olive oil

FOR THE TOPPING:
⅓ cup minced onion
3 tablespoons olive oil
3 cups broccoli florets, cut into
   1-inch pieces
1 tablespoon minced garlic

Salt
Pepper
3 tablespoons water
¼ pound smoked mozzarella,
   thinly sliced
½ cup drained and minced oil-
   packed sun-dried, tomatoes
Fresh whole basil leaves
2 tablespoons freshly grated Parmesan cheese

MAKE THE DOUGH: Proof the yeast in ½ cup warm water for 5 minutes, or until it is foamy.

In a food processor, combine 2 cups of the flour and the salt. With the motor running, add the yeast mixture, the olive oil, and the remaining ¼ cup warm water. Process the mixture until it forms a ball, adding more flour a little at a time, if necessary. Process for 20 seconds more to knead the dough. Turn the dough into an oiled bowl, making sure it is well coated with the oil on all sides. Let rise, covered with plastic wrap and a towel, in a warm place for 1 to 1 ½ hours, or until it is doubled in bulk.

Roll the dough into a circle ¼-inch thick and place it in an oiled pizza pan; if you don't have one, arrange it on an oiled heavy baking sheet.

Preheat oven to 450°.

MAKE THE TOPPING: In a skillet, cook the onion in 2 tablespoons of the oil, stirring over moderate heat for 3 minutes. Add the broccoli, garlic, and salt and pepper to taste. Cook, stirring, for 1 minute more. Add the 3 tablespoons water to the skillet, cover, and steam the broccoli for 3 minutes, or until just tender.

Spoon the broccoli mixture onto the dough, top it with the mozzarella cheese and sun-dried tomatoes, and garnish with the basil leaves. Sprinkle the pizza with the Parmesan, and drizzle the remaining oil over it. Bake in the lower third of the oven for 15 to 20 minutes, or until the cheese is melted and the crust golden brown. Serves 4 to 6.

TORTILLA PIZZA WITH BROCCOLI, ROASTED RED PEPPERS, AND CHEESE

. . . .

For lighter, quickly prepared individual pizzas, try these made with flour tortillas.

4 flour tortillas
2 tablespoons olive oil
1 small onion, minced
1 teaspoon ground cumin
Salt
Pepper
1 6-ounce jar roasted red peppers,
  drained and diced

2 cups blanched broccoli (p. 86),
  diced
1 cup grated Cheddar or Monterey
  Jack cheese
Minced fresh coriander

Preheat oven to 450°.

Brush the tortillas with 1 tablespoon of the oil and bake on a baking sheet in the oven for 2 minutes.

In a skillet, over moderate heat, cook the onion in the remaining oil, stirring occasionally, for 3 minutes. Add the cumin and salt and pepper to taste. Cook the mixture, stirring occasionally, for 3 minutes. Stir in the roasted red peppers and the broccoli and toss to combine.

Arrange the vegetables on top of the baked tortillas and sprinkle with cheese. Bake for 10 minutes, or until the cheese is melted and bubbling gently. Sprinkle with coriander to taste. Serves 4.

BROCCOLI AND CHEESE MELT

A simple, nourishing lunch.

2 tablespoons unsalted butter or
   margarine
½ cup thinly sliced scallions
2 cups broccoli, cut into 1-inch
   pieces
1 clove garlic, minced
Salt
Pepper
3 tablespoons water

1 to 2 tablespoons Dijon or coarse-
   grained mustard
4 slices whole-grain bread, lightly
   toasted
½ cup drained and sliced oil-
   packed sun dried tomatoes
4 thick slices cheese (Swiss, Monterey Jack, or Cheddar)

Preheat the broiler.

In a skillet, melt the butter over moderate heat. Add the scallions and cook, stirring occasionally, for 3 minutes. Add the broccoli, garlic, and salt and pepper to taste, and toss for 1 minute. Add the 3 tablespoons water, bring the liquid to a boil, and steam the broccoli, covered, for 2 to 3 minutes, or until tender.

Spread the mustard on one side of each slice of bread, cover with the broccoli mixture, and top with the sun-dried tomatoes and cheese. Broil 4 inches from the heat until the cheese is melted. Serves 4.

SIDE DISHES

SESAME BROCCOLI FLORETS

These make delightful nibbles and nutritious snacks. Pack them in plastic containers and add them to your picnic basket for a refreshing treat.

*3 cups blanched broccoli florets
(p. 86)
3 tablespoons rice or white wine
vinegar
2 tablespoons lite soy sauce
1 tablespoon Oriental sesame oil*

*2 teaspoons finely minced ginger-
root
1 teaspoon honey
Salt
Toasted sesame seeds for garnish*

Pat dry the broccoli. In a large bowl, whisk together the vinegar, soy sauce, sesame oil, gingerroot, honey, and salt to taste. Add the broccoli and toss to coat with the sauce. Let stand at room temperature, partially covered with plastic wrap, for 30 minutes. Sprinkle with the sesame seeds before serving. Makes 4 cups.

SAUTÉED BROCCOLI WITH GARLIC, LEMON, AND PINE NUTS

. . . .

This quick sauté is equally good hot or at room temperature. Almost any type of nuts may be used—pecans, walnuts, hazelnuts. For added flavor, toast the nuts in a 350° oven for 10 minutes, or until they have a rich, nutty aroma and are lightly colored.

3 tablespoons olive oil
1 tablespoon minced garlic
1 bunch broccoli (about 1½ pounds), separated into 2-inch florets, stalks peeled and cut into 1½-inch sticks, blanched (p. 86)

Salt
¼ teaspoon red pepper flakes
2 tablespoons lemon juice
¼ cup toasted pine nuts

Heat the olive oil in a large skillet over moderately high heat. Add the garlic, and cook, stirring, for 30 seconds. Stir in the broccoli, salt to taste, and red pepper flakes, and cook, stirring, for 1 to 2 minutes, or until it is heated through. Add the lemon juice and toss to combine. Transfer to a serving dish and sprinkle with the nuts. Serves 4 to 6.

BROCCOLI PUREE

. . . .

A smooth, creamy broccoli puree is sublime in itself—and need not be overly rich.

1 bunch broccoli (about 1½
pounds), separated into 2-inch
florets, stalks peeled and cut into
¼-inch slices
Freshly grated nutmeg
Salt

Pepper
1 tablespoon unsalted butter or
margarine, softened
¼ cup heavy cream or half-and-
half

In a large saucepan of boiling salted water, cook the broccoli over moderately high heat for 5 to 6 minutes, or until it is tender. Drain. In a food processor, puree the broccoli in batches until smooth. Add the nutmeg, and salt and pepper to taste. Transfer the broccoli to a saucepan and cook over moderate heat, stirring, until hot. Stir in the butter and cream and continue to cook until heated through. Serves 4.

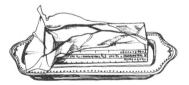

BROCCOLI GRATIN WITH BREAD CRUMBS AND PARMESAN

This dish may be prepared several hours in advance, covered with plastic wrap, and chilled. Bring back to room temperature before baking or add an additional 8 to 10 minutes to the baking time.

1 bunch broccoli (about 1½ pounds), separated into 2-inch florets, stalks peeled and cut into 1½-inch sticks, blanched (p. 86)
Salt
Pepper
3 tablespoons olive oil

2 teaspoons minced garlic
1 tablespoon minced fresh oregano or *thyme*, or 1 teaspoon dried
¼ cup dry bread crumbs
¼ cup freshly grated Parmesan cheese
2 tablespoons unsalted butter

Preheat oven to 400°.

Arrange the broccoli in a buttered shallow 1-quart baking dish and season with salt and pepper to taste. In a small saucepan, heat the olive oil over moderate heat. Add the garlic and oregano and cook over low heat, stirring, for 1 minute. Spoon the mixture over the broccoli and sprinkle with the bread crumbs and Parmesan. Dot with the butter. Bake in the oven for 20 minutes, or until the top is golden. Serves 4.

BROCCOLI PUFF

This is a beautiful dish that is simple to prepare and elegant enough to serve to guests.

6 cups broccoli, florets cut into
  4-inch pieces, stalks peeled
½ cup mayonnaise
½ cup freshly grated Parmesan
  cheese

2 teaspoons Dijon mustard
Pinch of cayenne
Salt
2 large egg whites, beaten until
  they hold firm peaks

Preheat oven to 350°.

Arrange the broccoli in a buttered shallow 1-quart baking dish. In a bowl, combine the mayonnaise, ⅓ cup of the Parmesan, the mustard, cayenne, and salt. Fold in the egg whites, gently but thoroughly, and spoon the mixture over the broccoli. Sprinkle with the remaining Parmesan and bake in the oven for 15 minutes. Serves 4.

BROCCOLI STIR-FRY WITH SESAME

A light, easy-to-make side dish that complements seafood, chicken, or beef.

2 tablespoons vegetable oil
1 tablespoon minced fresh gingerroot
2 teaspoons minced garlic
1 bunch broccoli (about 1½
  pounds), florets cut into 1½-
  inch pieces, stalks peeled and
  sliced

Salt
½ cup chicken stock or broth
1 tablespoon Oriental sesame oil
1 tablespoon toasted sesame seeds
  (optional)

Heat a wok or large skillet over moderate heat until it is hot, add the oil, and continue heating. When hot, add the gingerroot and garlic and stir-fry for 1 minute. Add the broccoli and salt to taste. Toss for 1 minute, or until it is bright green. Pour in the chicken stock, cover, and simmer for 2 to 3 minutes, or until just tender. Uncover, add the sesame oil, and toss. Transfer the broccoli to a serving dish and sprinkle with the sesame seeds, if desired. Serves 4.

STEAMED BROCCOLI

. . . .

1 bunch broccoli (about 1 ½
   pounds), tough stems and outer
   leaves removed

Melted butter or margarine
Salt
Pepper

Separate the broccoli into florets about 2 inches long; peel the stalks and either cut diagonally into ¼″ × 2″ sticks or slice diagonally. Arrange the broccoli in a steamer basket over boiling water and steam, covered, for 6 to 8 minutes, or until tender. Drain, transfer to a bowl, and toss with the butter. Season with salt and pepper to taste. Serves 4.

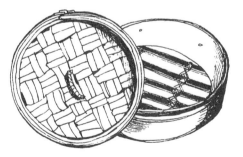

BLANCHED BROCCOLI

. . . .

1 *bunch broccoli, separated into*   *stalks peeled and cut into*
  florets about 2 inches long,   *2″ × ¼″ sticks*

To a large saucepan of boiling salted water, add the broccoli and cook over moderately high heat, stirring occasionally, for 3 minutes, or until it is just tender. Drain and refresh under cold running water.

SAUCES FOR BROCCOLI

CHEESE SAUCE

. . . .

If a lighter sauce is desired, substitute 1 ½ cups chicken stock *or* broth for 1 ½ cups of the milk. Add ½ cup milk to enhance the color of the sauce.

1 recipe Steamed Broccoli (p. 85)

FOR THE SAUCE:
1 small onion, finely minced
3 tablespoons unsalted butter or
  margarine
3 tablespoons flour

2 cups scalded milk
½ cup grated cheese (Swiss or
  Cheddar)
Freshly grated nutmeg
Salt
White pepper

Prepare the broccoli and arrange on a serving dish.

In a heavy saucepan, cook the onion in the butter over moderate heat, stirring occasionally, for 3 minutes. Add the flour and cook over moderately low heat, stirring, for 2 minutes. Add the milk in a stream, whisking, and simmer the sauce, stirring occasionally, over moderate heat for 10 minutes. Remove from heat and stir in the cheese, nutmeg, salt and white pepper to taste. Stir until the cheese is melted.

Spoon some of the sauce over the broccoli and serve the remaining sauce separately. Serves 4.

HOLLANDAISE SAUCE

For those special occasions when we wish to indulge . . .

1 recipe Steamed Broccoli (p. 85)

FOR THE SAUCE:
1 tablespoon white wine vinegar
2 tablespoons cold water

3 large egg yolks
10 tablespoons unsalted butter,
  melted
Lemon juice
Salt

Prepare the broccoli and transfer it to a serving dish.

In a small heavy saucepan, combine the vinegar and 1 tablespoon of the water; reduce the liquid to 1 tablespoon. Add the remaining tablespoon of cold water and the egg yolks and whisk the mixture over very low heat until it is thick enough for the whisk to leave a trail on the bottom of the pan. Whisk in the melted butter 1 tablespoon at a time, lifting the pan occasionally to cool the mixture, until it is thick. Add the lemon juice and salt to taste. Transfer the sauce to a sauceboat.

Serve broccoli accompanied by the sauce. Serves 4.

HORSERADISH CREAM SAUCE

. . . .

This is especially good with braised or boiled meats; delicious with brisket.

1 recipe Steamed Broccoli (p. 85)

FOR THE SAUCE:
3 tablespoons unsalted butter or
  margarine
3 tablespoons all-purpose flour

1½ cups scalded milk
¼ cup freshly grated horseradish,
  or to taste
½ to 1 teaspoon sugar
Salt
½ cup sour cream

Prepare the broccoli and transfer to a serving dish.

In a heavy saucepan, melt the butter over moderately low heat, add the flour, and whisk for 2 minutes. Add the milk in a stream, whisking, and simmer, stirring occasionally, for 5 minutes. Add the horseradish, sugar, and salt to taste, and continue to simmer for 5 minutes more. Stir in the sour cream and simmer for 2 minutes, or until heated through.

Spoon some of the sauce over the broccoli and serve the remaining sauce separately. Serves 4.

RÉMOULADE SAUCE

Light mayonnaise sauces are wonderful complementary accompaniments to broccoli. Here is just one. You might also try serving broccoli with a basil or green-herb mayonnaise, a mustard (coarse-grained) mayonnaise, or a sesame-oil mayonnaise.

1 recipe Blanched Broccoli (p. 86)

FOR THE SAUCE:
1 cup mayonnaise
2 teaspoons Dijon mustard
2 tablespoons minced capers
2 tablespoons minced pickled gherkins

2 tablespoons minced parsley
1 tablespoon minced chives or *scallions (green part only)*
1 teaspoon anchovy paste (optional)
Salt
Pepper

Prepare the broccoli and arrange it on a serving dish.

In a bowl combine the mayonnaise, mustard, capers, gherkins, parsley, chives, anchovy paste, and salt and pepper to taste and tranfer the mixture to a serving bowl.

Serve the broccoli with the sauce. Serves 4.

FLAVORED BUTTERS

. . . .

Below is a selection of seasoned butters that blend well with the flavor of broccoli. All are easy to prepare and may be made one to two days in advance. If desired, chill and cut into decorative shapes before adding to the broccoli.

FRESH HERB BUTTER:
1 stick unsalted butter or margarine, softened
2 tablespoons snipped fresh chives or scallions (green part only)
1 tablespoon minced parsley
2 teaspoons minced fresh tarragon, or ¼ teaspoon dried
Salt and pepper to taste

MUSTARD BUTTER:
1 stick unsalted butter or margarine, softened
½ teaspoon freshly grated lemon rind
1 tablespoon fresh lemon juice

1 to 2 tablespoons stone-ground mustard
Salt and pepper to taste

LIME-GINGER BUTTER:
1 stick unsalted butter or margarine, softened
2 teaspoons finely minced gingerroot
1 tablespoon lime juice
½ teaspoon freshly grated lime rind
Salt and pepper to taste

1 recipe Steamed or Blanched Broccoli (pp. 85–86)

FOR EACH BUTTER: Combine the ingredients, and if not using immediately, chill until ready to serve. Prepare the broccoli, transfer to a bowl, and toss with the butter. Serves 4.

INDEX

· · · · · · · · ·

Grains. *See also* Bulgur salad
. . . ; Rice

Ham, broccoli, and cheese
bread pudding, 51–52
Harissa, 49
Health benefits of broccoli,
4–5
Hollandaise sauce, 90
Hors d'oeuvres (broccoli,
chicken, and chili cheese
gratin), 39
Horseradish cream sauce,
91

Japanese miso and broccoli
soup, 14

Lamb and broccoli couscous,
49–50

Meat and broccoli, 47–54
beef enchiladas, 53–54
ham, broccoli, and cheese
bread pudding, 51–52
lamb and broccoli
couscous, 49–50
stir-fried with ginger and
mushrooms, 47–48
Meatless entrées, 69–75
Mushrooms and broccoli
with beef and ginger, 47
curried chicken, 40–41
and fusilli, 61

Panzanella (bread salad) with
broccoli, 19
Pasta and broccoli
with fresh tomato sauce, 66
frittata, 62–63
and mushrooms, 61
salad primavera, 17
Peanut sauce for vegetable
salad, 20
Peppers, broccoli, and cheese
on tortilla pizza, 74
Pizza, broccoli
with roasted red peppers
and cheese on tortilla, 74
with smoked mozzarella
and sun-dried tomatoes,
72
Popularity of broccoli, 4
Potatoes and broccoli
pie with ricotta and, 70
stuffed potato (broccoli and
shrimp), 30–31
Poultry, 37–44. *See also*
Chicken and broccoli;
Turkey and broccoli
Pudding, bread (broccoli,
ham, and cheese), 51–52
Pureed broccoli, 81

Quiche, broccoli and cheese, 69

Rémoulade sauce, 92
Rice and broccoli, 57–60,
64–65

casserole (brown rice),
59–60
pilaf with chick-peas and
tomatoes, 64–65
salad (brown rice), 18
with tomatoes, capers, and
olives, 58
Risotto with broccoli, 57

Salads with broccoli, 17–22
brown rice, 18
bulgur salad with
tomatoes, 21
dressings for, 18, 22
garden, 22
panzanella (bread salad),
19
tortellini salad primavera,
17
vegetable salad with peanut
sauce, 20
Sauces, 89–94
butters, flavored, 93–94
cheese, 89
dilled mustard cream,
43–44
hollandaise, 90
horseradish cream, 91
peanut, 20
rémoulade, 92
salad dressings, 18, 22
tomato, fresh, 66
Sautéed broccoli
and cherry tomatoes, 71